How Rock Climb

How to Rock Climb and Become the Best Rock Climber You Can Be From A to Z

HowExpert with Brigitte Ngo-Trinh

Copyright HowExpert™
www.HowExpert.com

For more tips related to this topic, visit HowExpert.com/rockclimbing.

Recommended Resources

- HowExpert.com – Quick 'How To' Guides on All Topics from A to Z by Everyday Experts.
- HowExpert.com/free – Free HowExpert Email Newsletter.
- HowExpert.com/books – HowExpert Books
- HowExpert.com/courses – HowExpert Courses
- HowExpert.com/membership – HowExpert Membership Site
- HowExpert.com/writers – Write About Your #1 Passion/Knowledge/Expertise & Become a HowExpert Author.
- HowExpert.com/resources – Additional HowExpert Recommended Resources
- YouTube.com/HowExpert – Subscribe to HowExpert YouTube.
- Instagram.com/HowExpert – Follow HowExpert on Instagram.
- Facebook.com/HowExpert – Follow HowExpert on Facebook.

COPYRIGHT, LEGAL NOTICE AND DISCLAIMER:

COPYRIGHT © BY HOWEXPERT™ (OWNED BY HOT METHODS). ALL RIGHTS RESERVED WORLDWIDE. NO PART OF THIS PUBLICATION MAY BE REPRODUCED IN ANY FORM OR BY ANY MEANS, INCLUDING SCANNING, PHOTOCOPYING, OR OTHERWISE WITHOUT PRIOR WRITTEN PERMISSION OF THE COPYRIGHT HOLDER.

DISCLAIMER AND TERMS OF USE: PLEASE NOTE THAT MUCH OF THIS PUBLICATION IS BASED ON PERSONAL EXPERIENCE AND ANECDOTAL EVIDENCE. ALTHOUGH THE AUTHOR AND PUBLISHER HAVE MADE EVERY REASONABLE ATTEMPT TO ACHIEVE COMPLETE ACCURACY OF THE CONTENT IN THIS GUIDE, THEY ASSUME NO RESPONSIBILITY FOR ERRORS OR OMISSIONS. ALSO, YOU SHOULD USE THIS INFORMATION AS YOU SEE FIT, AND AT YOUR OWN RISK. YOUR PARTICULAR SITUATION MAY NOT BE EXACTLY SUITED TO THE EXAMPLES ILLUSTRATED HERE; IN FACT, IT'S LIKELY THAT THEY WON'T BE THE SAME, AND YOU SHOULD ADJUST YOUR USE OF THE INFORMATION AND RECOMMENDATIONS ACCORDINGLY.

THE AUTHOR AND PUBLISHER DO NOT WARRANT THE PERFORMANCE, EFFECTIVENESS OR APPLICABILITY OF ANY SITES LISTED OR LINKED TO IN THIS BOOK. ALL LINKS ARE FOR INFORMATION PURPOSES ONLY AND ARE NOT WARRANTED FOR CONTENT, ACCURACY OR ANY OTHER IMPLIED OR EXPLICIT PURPOSE.

ANY TRADEMARKS, SERVICE MARKS, PRODUCT NAMES OR NAMED FEATURES ARE ASSUMED TO BE THE PROPERTY OF THEIR RESPECTIVE OWNERS, AND ARE USED ONLY FOR REFERENCE. THERE IS NO IMPLIED ENDORSEMENT IF WE USE ONE OF THESE TERMS.

NO PART OF THIS BOOK MAY BE REPRODUCED, STORED IN A RETRIEVAL SYSTEM, OR TRANSMITTED BY ANY OTHER MEANS: ELECTRONIC, MECHANICAL, PHOTOCOPYING, RECORDING, OR OTHERWISE, WITHOUT THE PRIOR WRITTEN PERMISSION OF THE AUTHOR.

ANY VIOLATION BY STEALING THIS BOOK OR DOWNLOADING OR SHARING IT ILLEGALLY WILL BE PROSECUTED BY LAWYERS TO THE FULLEST EXTENT. THIS PUBLICATION IS PROTECTED UNDER THE US COPYRIGHT ACT OF 1976 AND ALL OTHER APPLICABLE INTERNATIONAL, FEDERAL, STATE AND LOCAL LAWS AND ALL RIGHTS ARE RESERVED, INCLUDING RESALE RIGHTS: YOU ARE NOT ALLOWED TO GIVE OR SELL THIS GUIDE TO ANYONE ELSE.

THIS PUBLICATION IS DESIGNED TO PROVIDE ACCURATE AND AUTHORITATIVE INFORMATION WITH REGARD TO THE SUBJECT MATTER COVERED. IT IS SOLD WITH THE UNDERSTANDING THAT THE AUTHORS AND PUBLISHERS ARE NOT ENGAGED IN RENDERING LEGAL, FINANCIAL, OR OTHER PROFESSIONAL ADVICE. LAWS AND PRACTICES OFTEN VARY FROM STATE TO STATE AND IF LEGAL OR OTHER EXPERT ASSISTANCE IS REQUIRED, THE SERVICES OF A PROFESSIONAL SHOULD BE SOUGHT. THE AUTHORS AND PUBLISHER SPECIFICALLY DISCLAIM ANY LIABILITY THAT IS INCURRED FROM THE USE OR APPLICATION OF THE CONTENTS OF THIS BOOK.

**COPYRIGHT BY HOWEXPERT™ (OWNED BY HOT METHODS)
ALL RIGHTS RESERVED WORLDWIDE.**

Table of Contents

Recommended Resources..2
Chapter 1: Introduction - Spirit of Climbing..........................6
Why Climbing?... 6
Chapter 2: Intro to Climbing – Types of Climbing and Equipment 10
Bouldering..10
Top Rope..12
Sport Climbing...14
Traditional Climbing..15
Crack Climbing..17
Free Solo Climbing..19
Ice Climbing... 20
Chapter 3: Climbing Basics and Technique 101...................22
Knots and Belaying 22
    Figure 8 knot 22
    Double Fisherman's Knot 23
    Belaying 24
    Spotting.. 27
Hang Right not Tight! 28
It's All in the Feet and Legs! 31
Hips Don't Lie! 33
Dynos 36
Slab 40
Chapter 4: Training 43
CLIMB CLIMB CLIMB 43
Strength Training 45
    In the Weight Room 46
    Finger Strength... 47
Endurance Training 52
Chapter 5: Injury Prevention 56
Common Climbing Injuries 56
    Pulley Tears 56
    Rotator Cuff Tears 57
    Tendonitis and Tendinosis 58
    Partial Dislocation 59
Working Opposing Muscles 60
Tendons vs Muscles 62
Warm up, Cool Down, Stretch 63
    Warming Up 63
    Cool Down 66
    Stretching.. 67
Chapter 6: Be Polite, Don't be a Jerk - Climbing Etiquette 68
"Spraying Beta" and why it is a No No 68
LNT - Leave No Trace.. 69

First Come, First Serve *71*
Unwritten Rules of Climbing *76*
Chapter 7: Transitioning Outside **77**
Can I Climb Alone? *77*
Most Common Types of Rock *78*
   Granite 79
   Limestone 80
   Sandstone 80
   Volcanic.. 82
Multi-pitch and Big Wall Climbing *82*
The "Approach" *84*
Climbing After a Rainy Day *85*
ABC's of Climbing Index **88**
About the Expert **91**
Recommended Resources **92**

Chapter 1: Introduction - Spirit of Climbing

Why Climbing?

With 2020 being climbing's inaugural year in the Olympics, the sport seems to have had a huge influx of bodies in gyms and at the crag. We have seen exponential growth in the number of people wanting to try their hand at the sport. We are seeing climbers on commercials, in movies, and all over the internet. I can't tell people I'm a climber without at least 9 out of 10 people asking me if I've seen <u>Free Solo</u>. Yes, I have seen <u>Free Solo</u>. And No, I do not free solo. And No, that is not all climbing is. There is so much more to it than that. While climbing is a great way to get fit, there's so much more to climbing than building muscle and getting to the top. The process of climbing, while very physical, has a large mental component.

Climbing isn't just a sport, it is a community. A community of people you can, quite literally, trust your life with and who take it upon themselves to pass down valuable knowledge about the sport if you are willing to listen. It is then your responsibility to bestow this information on to the next newcomer and them to the next. But with this boom in the sport, there has been a shift in the tides. Newcomers are outpopulating the veterans, throwing themselves into climbing without taking the time to learn from the experts and the experienced. This disconnect is painfully apparent as we make the transition to the outdoors, and we see the lands being disrespected and trashed. **Climbing outside is a privilege, not a right.** How to climb is one thing, but the importance of etiquette, both indoors and outdoors. Let's start with why climbing is so great.

Every climbing problem or route is a puzzle that has a different solution for each individual. You can have all the muscle strength in the world, but if you don't figure out how to maneuver your body, you won't even leave the ground. A shorter person isn't going to be able to reach the same moves as a taller person. A taller person isn't going to fit in a position as comfortably as a shorter person. Some are better at using their feet and body, while others have the finger strength of the gods and can power through any hold. What is the best and most efficient way for **you** to get to the top? That is what you, the climber, have to figure out. What works for your friend might not necessarily work for you, and that is the beauty of climbing, the amount of thought put into each move on a climb.

When you walk into a climbing gym, you might see people staring at the wall, waving their hands around like mimes. They may look crazy, and you might be thinking "what a nut" but what they are doing is very strategic. They are reading the climb, imagining the movements, and planning their map to the top. If it doesn't work, it's back to the drawing board. Reading a climb is a skill, and a valuable one at that. Being able to read a climb before leaving the ground gives you that mental clarity to move up the rock like a dance, if done well. Like any other skill, it needs to be practiced; trial and error.

Climbing will teach you patience, and tenacity. Strong climbers are strong because they have been spit off the wall more times than they have made it to the top. It's a process, and you learn to love it. Every progression, no matter how small, is satisfying. And progress is never ending. Once you overcome one hurdle, there is another challenge waiting for you on the other side.

Climbing indoors is just practice and training for the real treat; the great outdoors. Something about being outside and in tune with nature brings on this sense of calm. Maybe it's all the green and fresh air. Maybe it's the peace and isolation. When you get to the top of a climb, whether it be a boulder problem or a long roped route, you are rewarded with breathtaking views, fresh air free of smog and a great sense of accomplishment. Nothing better than a pure serene calm to embrace you after the work and struggle to get there. If only that were true for every aspect of life! There's also something to be said about doing outdoor activities. For as exhausted as climbing is, the end of a climbing trip seems to always leave the climber feeling refreshed and recharged.

You won't find a more welcoming community. When someone decides that they want to climb with you or makes you their climbing partner, it is a big deal. That means they are trusting you with their life. Literally. On a rope, you are holding their life in your hands, and they 100% believe that you will safely help them to the top and help them back down. They trust in your ability to properly belay them. When bouldering, the climber is putting his/her faith in you to help them safely fall onto the crash pad in the even they blow off the wall. This is an aspect of climbing you won't find in any other sport, and because of this, the bond you build within the climbing community feels closer and tight knit. As a climber traveling around the world, you are immediately embraced by the community everywhere you go. Even if you start out as a climber just because you wanted a good workout, if you stick with it and become obsessed like so many have, you will inevitably feel like you are a part of a global club. It's pretty cool.

Let that sink in for a minute. Someone is trusting you, with their **life**. It is a huge responsibility. How many of you can say you have that weight on your shoulders on a day to day basis? While climbing is loads of fun, one has to remember that it can be dangerous if you take it lightly. You have to be sure you are prepared to take that responsibility. Be aware. Be mindful. Be present. Distractions can be lethal.

Chapter 2: Intro to Climbing – Types of Climbing and Equipment

Before you start climbing, it's good to know the different types of climbing. That way, you have an idea of what you would be interested in trying and have the proper equipment to try said style. The types of climbing will be listed from simplest form with the least amount of equipment to the most difficult and complex. You will hear these different terms often when climbing both in gyms and outdoors. Climbing doesn't have to be an expensive sport in its simplest form, but it can get pretty pricey the deeper you dive into the sport, as you will see in this chapter.

Bouldering

This style of climbing requires nothing but climbing shoes and a chalk bag. Originally starting out as a method of training for climbing longer routes by isolating specific and difficult moves close to the ground and building stamina and finger strength, the sport eventually evolved into its own discipline.

Boulder problems, as they are called, are usually no taller than 20 feet and are rated on a V scale in the US; V0 being the easiest and the higher the number, the higher the difficulty.

V0 (Easiest)	V1	V2	V3	V4	V5	V6	V7	V8	V9	V10+ (Hardest)

Europe uses the Fontainbleau scale. Each problem is assigned number and a corresponding letters a, b and c to indicate the difficulty.

4 Easiest	5	5+	6A / 6A+	6B / 6B+	6C / 6C+	7A	7A+	7B / 7B+	7B / 7C	7C+ < Hardest

Traversing is another bouldering training method that is commonly seen as a warm up.

- A traverse is the action of climbing sideways rather than climbing up. I will talk more about this in the training section of this book. Since bouldering has taken a life of its own, it has become one of the more popular forms of climbing due to its simplicity. A climber can go to the gym (or outdoors) by themselves with a pair of shoes and a chalk bag and hop on the wall, work on problems, and then go home.

When bouldering outside, it is recommended to have one more piece of equipment: a crash pad.

- A crash pad is a 3-4 inch foam landing mat that is placed on the ground under the climb. The purpose of this pad is to protect the climber in the event of falling. Placed under the climb, the crash pad, also known as a bouldering pad, is used to soften the landing in the event of a fall, cover any protruding rocks that could be extremely unpleasant to fall on, and they make great seats when they aren't being used to potentially save your life. Although bouldering outdoors alone is possible, it is not advisable. Anything could happen outside, and it is always safer to go with someone. This person will also be your "spotter". In addition to your crash pad, a spotter is someone who is watching you while you climb, and in the event of a fall, he or she will assist in directing your falling body towards the crash pad for a safe landing.

Think of bouldering as sprinting in the sport of climbing. It builds strength and power more so than endurance, which is why it began as a form of training rather an a sport on its own.

Top Rope

When transitioning to rope climbing, most people will start out with top roping, the simplest form of roping up. This type of climbing is exactly how it sounds, the rope is laced from the top of the climb before you attach yourself to it. Since the rope is coming from the top, if you fall on a top rope climb, you don't go anywhere as the rope is bearing your weight from above. This makes it easier to climb routes of harder grades without having to worry about the potential fall. Some advanced climbers do this to work on difficult parts of certain climbs to practice and dial in specific movements, this is called projecting. Before you start roping up, it is crucial that you learn the most important parts of climbing with a rope, how to tie yourself in, and how to belay. These aspects will be covered in Chapter 3 – Climbing Basics.

When climbing in a gym, top ropes will already be set throughout the rope area. You can walk up with a partner, tie yourself in, and up you go. On the other hand, ropes are not set up for you outdoors. If you are not an experienced climber, go with someone who knows what they are doing so that they can safely set things up for you. Normally, someone else will have to "lead" the climb to the top and set up an anchor which will allow the rope to feed through for a top rope to be set. In some cases, you can walk right up the back of the climb to set a top rope, but it is still highly recommended to have someone experienced do this, especially if an anchor has to be built. If you don't know any climbers, don't worry, the gym is a great place to meet people who are more than happy to take you under their wing.

Top Rope is the safest form of climbing with the least risk of injury. But don't let this give you a false sense of security. You still need to pay attention and not let yourself get distracted. This form of climbing uses the Yosemite 5.x scale. The higher the x, the more difficult the climb. If you are strictly climbing in the gym, you will need climbing shoes, chalk and a harness. If you plan on going outside, you might want to add a rope, belay device, and a few quick draws to your list of equipment.

Sport Climbing

Sport Climbing is a form of climbing that relies on permanent anchors that have been drilled into the rock for protection. This form of climbing requires the least amount of gear, sport climbing requires shoes, chalk, a harness, rope, a belay device and quick draws (can also be used to build anchors). Quick draws are composed of two carabiners attached by a strong webbing used to clip in to the permanent fixtures on the rock at one end and your rope at the other.

Lead climbing means you are climbing above your rope. You are "leading" your rope. As the climber, you tie yourself in to one end of the rope using the figure 8 knot (the most commonly used knot) and you start climbing, carrying all the gear you need to safely climb the wall. Off the ground to the first clip, you will essentially be bouldering as you are not attached to anything. Once you clip in to the first permanent clip with your quick draw and clip your rope in, you are officially on lead. Your partner, also known as your belayer, will be feeding you rope and is responsible for catching you when you fall. The fall is usually what makes the climber anxious when lead climbing. Unlike falling on top rope, where you barely move, falling on a sport climb can be a long way. However far you are from your last clip, you will fall double that. If you are 5 feet above your clip, you will fall 10 feet. If you are 10 feet above your climb, you will fall 20. So on and so forth, you get the picture.

Most sport climbs are very well protected with bolts pretty close to each other and with a good belayer you can focus on your breathing and movement. In the event you pop off the wall, your body naturally falls out, so the fall will be clean and you won't have to worry about scraping yourself on the way down. Just make sure your feet are on the outside of the rope, otherwise you run the risk of getting your foot wrapped in the rope. Rope burn sucks.

For this style of climbing, you will need: shoes, chalk, rope, quickdraws, locking carabiner, belay device, harness, and a helmet.

Traditional Climbing

Traditional climbing, also referred to as trad climbing or simply trad, is the next step up in lead climbing. In sport climbing, there are permanent anchors that have been drilled into the wall, but in traditional climbing, the wall is completely bare. This style of climbing requires the climber to place all the gear required to protect themselves in a fall. These pieces are then removed by the climber when the route is finished. The most common pieces of trad gear (on top of all the equipment listed thus far) are called cams, nuts and slings. A cam is a spring-loaded device that fits in a crack on the wall, and the opposing pressure against the rock locks the device in to hold your weight.

The cam is attached to a sling, also known as a runner – a strongly sewn loop of webbing, which is then clipped into a carabiner that the rope goes through. In many instances, slings are added to reduce "rope drag" allowing the rope to feed through smoothly with little resistance.

Nuts, made of aluminum, steel or brass, are wedges threaded through a metal wire that can be attached to quick draws. Like the cams, nuts come in a variety of sizes and what is needed is very specific to each climb. Placing a nut is best when a crack is decreasing in size and a piece can be wedged and locked into place.

Trad climbing isn't for the faint hearted. If a piece of equipment isn't placed properly, it could pop out when weighted. If it sounds scary, it is. It will definitely get your heart pumping. You will also have to get used to climbing with a decent amount of weight attached to you. Cams and nuts are not light in numbers and can hang awkwardly when you are climbing. Trad climbing will also require more endurance than any of the climbing described thus far because, on top of hauling up gear weighing as much as a small child, the climber will need to figure out which cam or nut is the correct size to fit in the area of placement, and if the climber is not practiced, it could take a few tries while hanging with one arm. A "run out" is another factor that can get the adrenaline kicking in. You will come to learn very quickly that, in climbing, adrenaline is not your friend. When someone says a climb is "run out" there are saying there is a long stretch of climbing where there is no solid spot to place gear, so a fall would receive little to no protection.

Traditional climbing is a much more advanced form of climbing that takes a lot of practice to get in the right headspace to remain calm through any situation. Adrenaline can be a climbers worst nightmare but once it is mastered, a whole new world of climbing will be open to you.

It's an investment... a single cam will start at about $60 minimum and a bare minimum starter trad climbing rack can set you back about $1000, and even then, you might not have all the pieces you need to climb the climb you want to climb. How many times can I say climb in one sentence? Hah! I recommend trying this out with some friends first before you decide if you want to take on this dent in your wallet.

Crack Climbing

Who loves crack? Do you love crack? Climbers sure do! Well... some do. Crack climbing is exactly how it sounds. You climb a crack. Not only will you be using your hands and feet to climb, you will be wedging any and every part of your body that will fit into the crack to shimmy your way up. There are about four classifications of crack sizes: finger cracks, hand cracks, off width cracks and chimney cracks: which is a crack that fits your entire body. A finger crack is just wide enough to fit the width of the fingers. "Finger locking" is a term used for sticking your finger or fingers in a crack and twisting downwards until your fingers feel locked into the crack. You'll know when you get it right, it will feel bomber - a term used by climbers to describe a hold that feels secure. Hand cracks are large enough to fit the entire hand ranging from a flat hand to a fist. Like finger locks, hand jams feel solid when you get them right. Off width cracks are wider than the hand but not quite wide enough for the legs or body. Generally, this type of crack tends to be really difficult to get through and requires some awkward and uncomfortable body positioning. Chimney cracks are large enough to fit an entire body and then some. What the crack size is classified as can depend on the size of the climber. A chimney crack for a 5 foot person may be an off width crack for someone who is 6 feet. A hand crack for a small child will be a finger crack for an adult and so on and so on. Confusing, I know. I've had a few conversations that went like this: "You get your whole hand in there? That's barely a finger crack for me!"

No crack climb is uniform in width. Most, if not all, crack climbs will require a person to use various techniques to get to the top. "Jamming" is the most fundamental technique in crack climbing and uses the friction created by the force of body part pressing against both walls in the crack. "Stemming" is a term used for a crack that is wider than the body and the force of limbs pressing outward creates the friction to stay on the wall. Crack climbing will require you to get creative in your technique of going up as the crack isn't always going to accommodate your body size. For protection, you will be using the same equipment as traditional climbing.

Free Solo Climbing

Yes, like the movie/documentary. If you haven't seen it, I mean, do you even climb bro? I'm kidding. But really though, if you plan on telling people you are a climber, be prepared to be asked if you know about "that movie with the one guy who climbed in Yosemite with no ropes, that's just insane" and you would answer, Alex Honold and "Free Solo". Honold is a free solo climber, which means he climbs routes (not boulders) that are more than 30 feet tall without using ropes. As you can imagine, this is the most dangerous form of climbing and requires absolute laser focus. A free soloist needs to be absolutely confident in their abilities to not only climb, but to climb whatever route they're about to ascend with zero protection. Zero. None.

There is no room for error. The most minor of slips can send you down to your death. It's terrifying, but insanely rewarding for those who have the mental game to do so. I'm going to tell you right now, I am not one of those people, but I admire those who do. The definition of free solo climbing is climbing without any aid or protection. Fully exposed to the elements, a free soloist is at the mercy their own coolheadedness and mother nature. Whether it's 5.6 or a 5.14, anything could happen, so if you do decide to test your hands at a little free solo, make sure your head is fully in the game, even then there are forces out of your control. Some of the most famous and best free solo climbers in the world met their untimely demise not because they lack the skill, but because of forces beyond their control. Currently, the most famous free soloist is Alex Honold. His predecessors include John Baccar, Dan Osmond, Wolfgang Gullich, and many others, most of whom (including the three mentioned) are no longer with us. Do you have the mental fortitude?

Ice Climbing

Exactly how it sounds; climbing on ice. You might be wondering, how the heck do you climb ice? It's freezing and your hands would go numb. You're right, it would, if you were using your hands to make your way up these spires of solid glaciers or frozen waterfalls colder than the ice in your freezer. Ice climbing is similar to rock climbing except the terrain is completely different which calls for different equipment to ascend the icy walls. Evolving out of climbers' and mountaineers' need to navigate icy and slippery zones on their way up a mountain or rock wall, special tools were created and over time ice became its own discipline in the sport. As you might have guessed, rubber climbing shoes aren't going to fare well in these conditions. For this reason crampons were invented. Crampons are fittings that attach to boots with sharp fangs sticking out of the front acting like claws latching on to the ice. Ice axes are used as extensions of your hands. The sharp tip is used to chisel and hang on to the ice as the climber makes their way up.

Similar to rock climbing, the climber can lead or follow. Both the leader and follower will tie in with a most commonly used figure 8 knot on either end and climb as they would a multi-pitch climb (explained later in this book). The leader will need to screw in their own protection, called ice screws, on their way up, and the follower will remove the gear when it is their turn to go up. Ice screws are tubular screws that run about 10-20+ cm long and can withstand approximately 7 kilo Newtons of force.

Ice climbing is not for the faint hearted. Take all the dangers of rock climbing and add in the sub zero temperatures, potentials for avalanches, wondering if you'll get frostbite, and all the risks that come with being at high elevation. There is a lot that goes in to ice climbing. It is recommended to learn from and go with expert and experienced climbers in this field. Mixed climbing is a combination of both rock and ice climbing. That's a lot of gear to carry!

Chapter 3: Climbing Basics and Technique 101

There is a difference between being a stronger climber and being a better climber. Strength can come and go and plateau, but if you have the right technique, it will stay with you forever. You want to be the better climber. Build your technique, strength can come later.

Knots and Belaying

Figure 8 knot

A figure 8 knot is the most common knot used in all of climbing. When tying a figure 8 knot, every line in the knot is doubled up as shown below:

Here are the steps to make a perfect figure 8 knot:

1. About 2-2.5 feet from the end of the rope, fold the rope over so that the two sides are parallel with a loop on top
2. Grab the top of the loop and twist the rope once so that there is an X formed under the loop, then twist it one more time back to its original position
3. Take the piece of rope on the right (the short end) and thread the end of the rope through the loop from behind (rope tip threading towards your face) and pull it through for the first part of the figure 8

4. Thread the same end through your tie-in loops on your harness and feed the rope back through the knot, tracing the original knot as you go. You want the working end to run completely parallel with the standing end.
5. Once you have checked and the strands are neat and parallel, you can tighten the knot

Double Fisherman's Knot

After you finish tying your figure 8 knot and are securely fastened, as a precautionary measure, a double fisherman's knot is used as a safety knot to tie off what is left of the rope. There are many types of safety knots used depending on who you ask, but the most commonly used, and the one that will be taught in almost all gyms is the double fisherman's knot which looks like this:

1. After tightening your figure 8 knot, hold the running end and the standing end parallel with each other.
2. About 3 inches up, wrap the working end around the parallel strands twice.
3. Thread the running end through both of the loops you have created and pull tight.

Now that you are securely fastened to the rope, you are ready to climb! When it comes time to switch with your partner, you will now be the "belayer". You are in charge of the safety of your partner. In short, their life is literally in your hands, so make sure you know exactly what you are doing, or you have someone watching you and assisting you.

Belaying

As a belayer, you are quite literally holding your partner's life in your hands. Let that sink in again for the second time in this book and feel the weight of the responsibility that comes with it. This is not to be taken lightly, no matter how confident or safe you feel. I have seen some of the most veteran climbers make mistakes or have slip ups because they become complacent and just go through the motions. No matter how experienced you are, you have to be diligent.

There are some key terms you will need to know. **Take** – tension is also used- means tighten the rope. When you hear this, you will take in all the rope there is until the rope is tight and the climber is sitting on the wall, using your weight as the anchor. **Slack** – to give rope. **Falling** - the climber is about to take a fall. Easy right? You will hear this a lot in lead climbing when you are feeding the climber rope as they go up. If you have the rope too tight while climbing, the climber will have a difficult time moving up and clipping in. If the rope is too tight when the climber takes a fall, they will slam into the wall, and probably never let you belay them again. That's just asking for a foot injury. What you want to do is to give your partner a **soft catch**. Aside from knowing how to properly use your belaying device, giving a soft catch is one of the most important techniques of belaying.

A soft catch lengthens the fall, making the final catch less jaring.

Note: a soft cath does **NOT** mean you give a lot of slack.

- How do you give a soft catch?
    - Only allow as much slack as necessary (enough for the climber to make the clip without having to forcefully tug on the rope)
    - Stand straight: don't lean back or lean forward. If the climber falls, you will be pulled in towards the wall, be ready
    - Soft bend in the knees: don't lock out your legs
    - Hop: this requires precise timing. If you hop too soon, you risk coming down too soon and weight the rope making it taut. If you hop too late, you missed your window of easing the fall. As soon as you feel the fall, you need to hop.
    - Practice, practice, practice, this is an important and difficult skill to master

You'll know you gave a good soft catch if the climber barely swings when the rope catches.

- When would you not give a soft catch?
  - If the climber is at risk of hitting a ledge, a bulge, or the ground
  - If the landing is bad
  - If the climber only has one clip in

Weigh the safety options, and decide if it is necessary to minimize the length of the fall.

Before the start of the climb, the belayer will check all the knots and harnesses to make sure everything is good to go. MAKE SURE ALL THE GEAR IS SET UP PROPERLY BEFORE CLIMBING!

ALWAYS ALWAYS ALWAYS have both hands on the rope, no matter what type of belay device you are using, this is just good practice. Remember, the climber's life is in your hands. One hand, the guide hand, will be on the climber's end of the rope, and the other will be on the standing end of the rope as the brake hand. Under NO circumstance should the brake hand ever leave the rope.

If you are belaying for top rope, the rope will slacken as the climber goes up. You will pull the slack with the hand holding the climber's end of the rope then pull it through the belay device with your brake hand and locking the rope by pulling it tight by your hip. To move your brake hand closer to the belay device, use your guide hand to grab the brake rope. You are now able to safely move your brake hand closer to the belay device as your guide hand has become the intermittent brake hand. Repeat these steps until the climber is at the top.

Since you will be spending most of your time taking in slack, the most common technique for belaying on top rope is known as the PBUS belaying motion:

- **Pull** - Pull rope down with your guide hand while simultaneously pulling rope through the belay device with the brake hand
- **Brake** - When the rope is through, the brake hand goes down towards the hip to lock the rope in the device
- **Under** - Move the guide hand to the brake rope under the brake hand and grip firmly
- **Slide** - Slide the original brake hand back above the guide hand, grip the rope and move the guide hand back to its original position
- **Do it all over again**

Techniques for lowering the climber will depend on the type of device you are using. The basics for belaying a lead climber is the same as far as hand placements go, but instead of taking in rope, you will be feeding rope to the climber.

Spotting

Bouldering doesn't use a rope, or a harness, and all you have is a landing pad and a spotter for safety. What is a spotter? A spotter is someone who makes sure you land safely on the pad when you take a fall. You could have one or multiple spotters. The climber is, again, trusting you, so you need to be attentive and don't half ass it.

As a spotter, you will be in charge of pad placement and moving the pad around to make sure it is in the climbers landing zone. The zone can change as the climber moves. You need to be able to spot this and make necessary adjustments. Be aware of the landing zone and surroundings. When you are not adjusting the pads, you need to be prepared to catch the climber if/when they fall. Even if you don't think the climber is going to fall, be ready for it, you never know.

The Art of Spotting

1. Stand with one foot in front of the other with knees slightly bent. You will be using your body like a spring to absorb the shock of the fall
2. Arms up and slightly bent. Same concept as the legs. The bend will act as a spring to absorb the fall
3. Thumbs in. Imagine your hands are giant scoops with no space or gaps between fingers (and thumbs). This will prevent any one finger from being jammed back
4. Aim for the climbers center of gravity (hips, butt, waist) and guide them to the ground
5. Be aware of your surroundings. Keep the landing zone clear for your safety and the safety of the climber

Hang Right not Tight!

Now that we have the important safety part out of the way, let's get to the fun stuff, the actual climbing! As a new climber, you're going to hear a lot of people say "Hang on your bones!" This means that when the climber rests he/she hangs loosely on the arm/arms as to conserve muscle energy. While the idea behind the saying is a good rule of thumb, it isn't a good idea to completely hang on your bones. Hanging completely on your bones, over time, will cause undue stress, wear and tear on your shoulder and elbow joints and the tissue surrounding those areas, so while hanging, engage only the necessary muscles to protect your precious joints as these are prime sites for injury.

Muscles surrounding the shoulder should always be activated and engaged. Think about when you are lifting weights. When the bar is on the ground, you bend over to grab the bar, you wouldn't just lift with limp shoulders, it would feel like you're ripping the bone from its socket. Instead, you roll your shoulders back and down squeezing your scapulas together and engaging your back muscles, some of the largest muscles in the body. Climbing is similar; your body is a weight you will have to carry the entire time you are climbing and is heavier than the dumbells found in a gym.

Whether you are climbing or resting on the wall, it is best to do so with straight arms. Your arms have small muscles that tire easily, so you want them to be as relaxed as possible. If you are constantly engaging your arm muscles, they will tire quickly. Like in many sports, the more relaxed you are, the more you can get out of your muscles. How hard you are gripping is directly correlated to the amount of tension in the arms and your endurance on the wall. "Over gripping", a common mistake made with new and seasoned climbers, happens when a climber gets put in a position that causes them to be anxious or scared and they hold on too tightly to the hold. When you over grip, all of the muscles in your arms contract. Not just the tendons and fibers in your hands and fingers, but your forearms are going to take the brunt of the exhaustion.

Climbing already puts a lot of strain on your forearms as your fingers don't have muscles themselves. Bones in the fingers are held together by tendons and ligaments, which are then connected to the muscles in the palms, which is why it is such a slow process to build finger strength. The tendons in your fingers ultimately lead to the muscles in the forearms, so how you grip a climbing hold directly affects those muscles. So, the idea is to reduce the amount of work the forearms have to do by improving on how much energy we put into gripping the hold. The more relaxed the grip, the less work the muscles have to do. When you are climbing, practice climbing with the least amount of effort needed to get you up the climb. Practice gripping the hold just enough to keep you on the wall.

Remember, over gripping not only uses unnecessary energy and will exhaust you quicker, it can also be detrimental to your fingers, especially on the smaller holds. I'll reiterate because I find this to be very important, you're fingers do not have muscles as reinforcements. Tendons are much more fragile and take longer to strengthen and heal, so be gentle with them and don't put any excessive stress on them, or you'll be sitting on the side lines.

To sum it up, what to take away from this section is: climb with straight arms, engage your shoulders, and grip the holds with only as much energy is required to keep you on the wall.

It's All in the Feet and Legs!

The most common excuse from people who think they can't climb is. "I have no upper body strength." Believe it or not, a lot of climbing is in the legs. This is going to be a very obvious answer, but which appendage has bigger muscles, the arms or legs? If you said arms, you should google human anatomy... Legs are the powerhouses of the human body and are probably 4 times the size of arms. Based on sheer size alone, it makes sense for the legs to hold more and larger muscles. Look at almost every person around you. Only some of them work out, but all of them are able to carry their weight, walk around from place to place every day at all hours of the day. Flip them upside down, and 3-5% of them can do a handstand without the assistance of a wall. With appendages like those, why would anyone muscle their way up a climb doing pull up after pull up? Use your legs!

Climb as if you have never done a pull up in your life. There is a saying in climbing, and it is in no way meant to be sexist; "climb like a girl." Before you scorn me, there is scientific reasoning behind this. Women carry most of their strength in their legs while men are stronger in the upper body. There is a whole science behind it if you are interested in looking it up. It's not to say women can't build that strength, I'm just saying that men have a head start in that department, but in the case of climbing, it isn't always an advantage, especially in the beginning stages of climbing. While hanging on the hold with your straight arms and engaged shoulders, instead of pulling yourself up, push yourself up with your legs and use your arms as balance. The most fundamental and basic technique of climbing is pushing yourself up the wall, not pulling. For you rowers out there, you understand this concept very well. Push with your legs first; and the arms come after.

Start with easier climbs in the beginning so that you can take your focus off the arms, even if you think you can muscle up some of the harder ones. Some of the easier climbs are going to feel like ladders, and while they are not fun, it will allow you to concentrate on your legs as the driving force. Like walking up the stairs or a ladder, you use your hands as balance and move up with each step. Keep those arms straight and push with those legs. Exaggerate those movements and strengthen those micro muscles you've never used before until the movement feels natural.

Precise foot placement will help you conserve energy and train your mind and body to trust what you are standing on. Your feet shouldn't make noise when you place them on a hold. Climbers even made a drill out of it called quiet feet. Instead of flailing your legs around trying to slam your foot on a small chip, foot placement should be deliberate, regardless of which part of the foot you are using. Once you have placed your foot, keep it still, apply weight and pressure to ensure you don't slip off the wall or pop off the hold. When placing a toe, think of keeping your heel low so that you have the most contact with the wall as possible. This downward pressure will be the main point of the driving force pushing you up the wall.

When placing a heel, engage your hamstrings and pull your heel towards your body.

Make a game out of it. Starting with the lower grades, don't let yourself move on to the next climb or the next grade until you finish the one you are on without making a sound. Think delicate feet. An added little tip: it will be easier to quietly place your feet if you hang with straight and relaxed arms rather than locked off and bent arms. Not only will this conserve energy and take the focus of the arms, but the straight arms will allow for more space to find exactly where the placement needs to be and to comfortably set the foot.

Climbing with your legs and using precision feet will improve your climbing efficiency and prepare you to effectively climb harder moves in the long run. Next time someone says you climb like a girl, take it as a compliment.

Hips Don't Lie!

If you watch some of the best climbers, they are almost never square with the wall, even if the climb is like a ladder. When climbing, the goal is to make the movements as easy and effortless as possible, and to do this the climber needs to be closer to the wall. Bringing the body closer to the wall will bring the weight over the feet, taking some weight off the arms so that you are less likely to blow off the wall.

Well... if you are supposed to keep your arms straight, how do you sit on your feet AND push up the wall without bending your arms? By shifting your hips. Bringing your hip closer to the wall when making the next move not only brings your weight over your feet, but allows the shoulders to come closer to the wall, changing the angles of the pull on the holds. Now, the climber has angle and weight working in their favor. Have I lost you? Take a look at the images below.

Benefits of climbing with hips in the wall:

- You feel lighter on the wall - your weight is now over your feet taking some stress off the arms
- Lengthens your reach - a hold that you would have to go dynamically to being square to the wall can be reached statically by a simple turn of the hips. Whichever hand you want to move with, the corresponding hip should be flush with the wall. Want to move up and to the right? Weight and hang on the left arm to keep you on the wall, turn so that the right hip is flush with the wall, push with the right leg and extend the right arm to grab the hold. The opposite will be true if movement is to be made with the left hand
- You look really cool and graceful on the wall and making better use of your energy

The key to climbing is to be comfortable and confident on the wall, and the best way to achieve that is finding balance and being solid in every move. Most climbs aren't going to be straightforward and will require combinations of lateral and upward movements.

Holds are going to be pointing in different directions and body movement is going to be crucial. Since your hips are your center of gravity, where you put them dictates your sense of balance on the wall. You are going to run into a plethora of holds of different sizes at different angles, and how you position your body can dictate how you feel on each of those holds.

For example, when there is a hold that is pointed to the side, pressure going the opposite direction will need to be applied in order to counter the force of the "side pull" so that you won't be swinging off the wall.

- Say you grab a side pull with your left hand, you will want your weight to be going right to stay on the wall, but if you have your left foot on the wall, all the weight from your right side will come swinging left. Instead, you put your right foot on the wall, turn so that your right hip is up against the wall, and you push with your right leg as a counter balance. Not only does this help with feeling secure on the wall, this position will make the next move seem closer and easier.

This is the most efficient method of climbing and you'll expend the least amount of energy by using your body weight in your favor rather than against you. Instead of relying purely on strength to stay on the wall, gravity is giving you a chance to rest and relax the muscles that don't need to be engaged. Taking advantage of this, you will find moments where you can rest and shake out your arms.

This isn't going to be easy at first. Even though experienced climbers make it seem effortless, it takes practice. These movements engage muscles that aren't often used in most sports and will need to be trained often before it feels easier and becomes second nature. To practice this, when climbing, always try to keep one hip against the wall with every move to build that core strength.

A good drill for this technique involves finding a large hold for your hands with a foot hold directly underneath. The distance between the holds will depend on your height. Make sure you can hang with bent knees. Starting in a hang with one foot on the hold and the other foot flagged – straight and engaged, turn the hip into the wall and push to the next hold of your choice. Do this 10 times before switching to the opposite side. Repeat the drill as often as you'd like.

Dynos

Sometimes, there will be holds that cannot be reached statically and will require a big dynamic move to get to. In climbing, there are various types of dynamic movements: a lunge- where a minimum of two points are still in contact with the wall, a jump – always one point of contact where one hand stays on while both feet leave the rock, and a full on dyno – a giant leap leaving your entire body airborne with no points of contact on the wall.

Let's face it, dynos just look cool. Going airborne and latching on to a hold without being completely spit off the wall is probably one of the most satisfying feelings. It is the closest a human can feel to flying. Sometimes they are necessary on a climb, other times it's a fun party trick. Most of the time, it is a lot of flailing and falling and laughing. You see dynos a lot more in bouldering and younger climbers, mostly in climbing gyms, as it can take a toll on the body. If you can imagine, your full body weight is a lot of strain on your fingers and joints, especially if a dyno is caught with just one arm. You throw, you catch, and you have to control the swing. Be careful if you plan on attempting a dyno. Make sure all your joints are warm and ready to take on that load.

When watching climbers dyno, a technical term for dynamic movement where all points leave the rock, it may just look like they are swinging and jumping up to the next hold that seems to be a million miles away when you are sitting under it, but it's more than just throwing your body around in hopes you go far enough. A dyno isn't simply throwing yourself up the wall, there is a technique to it, and it's all in your... you guessed it... hips.

- A well-executed dyno will use less energy and power than static moves, but it is less controllable, which is why it is a better idea to reserve this kind of movement for out of reach holds.

The dyno takes less than a second to do, but within that second, every part of your body has to be working in sync to pull off the move. It will take a good amount of practice to get down the coordination. There are three phases to a proper dyno:

- **Set up** – All of the momentum of the dyno is going to be generated from the legs, so you want to sink down to generate the maximum amount of momentum needed to reach the target. First, choose foot holds that will solidly keep you on the wall. If there aren't many to choose from, choose the best ones you can find. The further the target is, the higher the feet should be. Think of a jump squat, the closer your center of gravity is to your feet, the more force you can generate for your jump. Once your feet are set up, sink down and straighten your arms. Your legs are going to be the spring that launches you up. Your arms are going to help you keep your body close to the wall so you don't go flying back.
- **Launch** – For the launch, you will be straightening your legs and pulling with your arms at the same time. Here's the important part, your hips are the driving force. You don't want to go flying off the wall backwards, but to stay close to the wall, so you want to be sure to drive your hips – center of gravity – towards the wall as you are going up. Make sure your hands finish their part in driving the momentum before letting go. A common mistake in a dyno is letting go of the hands too

early and falling off the wall before the dyno can even happen.
- **Latch** – Usually the hardest part of the dyno is holding on and controlling the swing as all points have left the rock and you are relying on the one hand (in some cases, both hands) to stay on. If you catch the hold with one hand, match with your other hand as quickly as possible. When catching a dyno, don't catch with limp arms. Be sure to have the muscles in your arms and shoulders engaged to protect the tendons and joints in your elbow and shoulder. A trick to slow down the momentum once latched is a slow long deep breath out that contracts the muscles in the abdomen.

The biggest part about a dyno, is the confidence. When you, the climber, feels unsure about whether you can make the move or latch on, chances are, you won't. That apprehension is going to make your body tense, or you won't push hard enough, or you let go too early, or you don't commit when you hit the hold. Mentally, if you're not prepared, the other steps won't amount to much. YOU CAN DO IT!! GET PSYCHED!! Dyno's can be a lot of fun and are very satisfying when done right. I recommend practicing dynos in a safe environment like a climbing gym before you try them outside. Start with small and gradually increase the distance of the jump. There will also be a lot of falling when it comes to practicing a dyno, so you'll get a good laugh.

Here are a few situations where dynos should be avoided.

- If there is potentially a sketchy fall, it is best to make the move statically to have better control of the move.
- If the target hold is one that requires precision, like a crack, or micro crimp for example.
- If the rock is very unforgiving, catching the hold at dynamic speeds can tear up your hand.

Throwing yourself on a move can be very dangerous. If you can't hang on, it can lead to a very awkward fall. If you do hang on, catching a hold at those speeds can be a heavy load on your fingers, tendons and joints, especially in the elbows and shoulders. Make sure the area under you is well padded and you have a good spotter. Also be sure to practice caution and make sure your warmed up for the move.

Slab

In front of you is a large rock, slightly less steep than vertical, and it looks completely blank aside from scattered chalk marks that look like they were put there to trick you. Welcome to slab climbing, one of the most technically demanding styles of climbing. Slab climbing calls for intense concentration, precise foot placement is extremely balancy, static and friction dependent. Movements are slow and smooth while steps are short and deliberate. Any jerky or dynamic movements will result in your foot popping off.

Unlike traditional climbing where you want your hips close to the wall, in slab climbing, your butt will be sticking out to keep you center of gravity directly over your feet maximizing friction. Having your weight close to the wall will push your feet off the wall.
"Nose over your toes," a popular slab mantra and good rule of thumb. Hands will be used to assist in balancing and pushing against the wall as there won't be a holds large enough to hang off of.   Think of using your palms to press instead of your fingers to grip.

Slab climbing revolves around a technique called smearing. Smearing is the art of placing the foot on a featureless spot on a rock and applying pressure, creating friction between the rubber on the shoe and the rock, to stay on. Going back to body positioning, this is why having your full weight over your feet is so important; more weight, increased friction. Surface area is also key in increasing friction. Rather than using just the tip of your toe for contact, lower your heels to put as much of the rubber in contact with the rock as possible. Your heels should be lower than your toes. Calculate every move, and avoid large movements (and high stepping) as they throw off your center of gravity. Use your breath to hone in your focus and stay calm.

The scariest part biggest mental hang up about slab of climbing is the fall. Falling on slab can cause some serious skin injury as it could lead to sliding and tumbling down the rock. In the community, we call it "cheese gratering". The fall isn't clean - dropping through the air and hanging - like it is on vertical or overhanging walls. If you pop off, try to stay upright and slide down as opposed to tumbling.

Chapter 4: Training

CLIMB CLIMB CLIMB

When you are starting out, the best way to get better at climbing is to just keep climbing. As a beginner, even if you have the muscle strength to do any sort of training, your tendons are not well enough adapted to carry the load. Build a solid foundation first, strength will come.

Tendons are significantly more fragile than muscles. If a muscle is torn, it will grow back stronger. That is the nature of how stronger muscles are built. A torn or strained tendon will not bounce back like muscles and won't fully heal. Have you ever sprained an ankle? It's never back to 100% and is always at risk of being sprained again. A tendon injury will be something you will have to be cautious of for the life of your climbing career. Work the muscles, baby the tendons.

That being said, if you can barely get up a V1 climb, it is not a good idea to jump on a crimp that is the size of a credit card or do finger board training at risk of popping tendons. From experience, I can tell you it is not worth it. Impatience leads to injury, work your way up! How do you build the tendon strength slowly? Just keep climbing. Here is an example of a climbing day:

Warm Up – Stretch and move to get the blood flowing. Then pick a few climbs that are well below your climbing ability and climb them slowly, using the wall to stretch the legs, arms and fingers. Do this for a minimum of 4-5 boulder problems or 3-4 roped routes to ensure that the muscles and tendons are warm and ready for the stresses that are about to be applied. Take your time during the warm up, it is the most important part of the climbing day. From here, start working climbs up to the grade you can climb.

Climb Time — Now that the body is sufficiently warm, you can start working on harder problems. A good friend of mine, a professional climber, once told me that if you want to consistently climb whatever grade you are working on, train on climbs that are 1 to 2 grades higher. The raise in difficulty is enough to challenge the climber, but not so much that it will subject them to moves that are completely out of their wheelhouse.

- For example: On boulders, you are a V1 climber who gets MOST V1s but not all. After warming up and working on a couple V1s, try a couple v2s and v3s. On rope, you are a 5.9 climber, try working on a 5.10a or 5.10b.

This will strengthen your tendons at a safe rate. We will discuss more about this in injury prevention later on.

Cool Down — Another crucial part of the climbing day that is almost always forgotten. Having done some hard climbs, your body is going to feel tired and stiff. Hop back on an easy climb and slowly make your way up, stretching the muscles you used, and cool your body down. You can also do this on the floor by stretching. This will relax your muscles and release any lactic acid that has built up during your session.

This method of "training" is also effective in all levels of climbing, not just in the beginning. A runner runs faster by running more and pushing their limits. It is the same concept here. You will effectively get stronger and better (two different things in climbing) by climbing more and challenging yourself. But also like any other sport, at a certain point, climbing alone can only get you so far, so strength training is incorporated.

Strength Training

Strength building in climbing can be divided into two areas; finger strength and the rest of the body. Building strength in climbing isn't like going to the gym and pumping iron like a bodybuilder. Building bulky muscles and getting bigger is a great disadvantage to a climber. Climbers want to also be light as well as strong. What climbers want to build is functional strength that will allow them to stay on the wall longer and move more efficiently. Remember this, building strength is supplemental to climbing. Technique is invaluable. Adding strength to poor technique is essentially reinforcing poor technique. The idea behind strength training is that a stronger climber will use less of their maximum strength to perform a move as to not compromise technique and to be more resistant to fatigue. Now, let's get into how to build strength for climbing.

In the Weight Room

In conjunction with climbing, a quick session in the weight room a couple times a week will give you that extra umph you need and teaches the body how to recruit all the muscle groups during movement. Since you are only going to be in the weight room a couple times a week, it is possible to focus on all the major muscle groups in one session. The sessions aren't long, but they are heavy. Don't fear the heavy! If you keep the reps to a total of 10 of heavy lifting, you will get stronger, but not heavier. By heavy, I don't mean you are completely winded after doing one set of 3. Heavy means difficult enough to feel the burn, but after finishing 3 sets of 3 with perfect form, you may have enough in the tank for another set. These sets aren't to failure. You aren't looking to be an olympic powerlifter, you simply want functional strength to supplement your climbing. Strength training will also help in preventing some of the most common injuries seen in climbing.

During your weight room workout, you will be focusing on 4 major movements

1. Hip Dominant - Deadlift
2. Knee Dominant - Squat
3. Pull
4. Press

Since climbing is reliant on mobility, each exercise will be coupled with a stretch. As outlined by Steve

Bechtel in his book <u>Climb Strong: Logical Progression</u>, a simple workout will look like this:

1. Deadlift - 3 reps
2. Frog Stretch - 60 seconds
3. Military Press - 3 reps
4. Shoulder Dislocates - 60 seconds
5. Front Squat - 3 reps
6. Hip Flexor Stretch - 30 seconds each side
7. Inverted Row - 3 reps
8. Y-Extension - 10 reps

Go through all of the exercises once through before repeating. Repeat the set 3 times.

There are many lifts and stretches that can be used for this workout, I just picked the most common ones for this example.

Finger Strength

How hard you can climb greatly depends on not only your technique and muscle strength, but also the strength of the tendons in your fingers. You could have the back muscles of the gods, gigantic shoulders, and arms like tree trunks, but without fingers like biceps, it might be difficult to even get your butt off the ground on some of these climbs,

First off, know that there are no muscles in your fingers, only tendons that attach to the muscles in the hands and forearms. Unfortunately, unlike muscles, tendons take much longer to strengthen and are much more fragile and susceptible to injury if pushed too far beyond its limits. So in the beginning, simply climbing more is going to be the best strategy to gain finger strength. Bouldering in particular since this discipline of climbing focuses on short problems and hard moves. Once you progress to more difficult climbs, you might find that perpetual climbing isn't going to get your fingers strong enough to make the necessary moves. This is when you make your way over to the hang board and campus board.

Hangs will build the isometric/static strength of your fingers - ability to hold static positions. The campus board will build more dynamic movements. This form of training is for more advanced training and should only be considered if you are an advanced climber, otherwise there is great risk at injuring yourself. Think of the hangboard as strength building, and the campus board as power training. Finger strength training is going to be at maximum effort, but be sure to exercise caution. I would not recommend serious finger training unless you climb in the V4-V5 range consistently or at minimum 2 years from when you first start climbing to allow your tendons to adapt.

Let's begin with the hangboard. If this is your first time training your fingers, keep the workout simple. Pick about 6 holds you can hang on with an open hand. Find holds that you can hold on to for about 10 seconds. If it feels like you can hang onto the hold for more than 10 seconds, the hold is too easy. Holding with an open hand means you can hang on with the least amount of effort. The second joint on your finger will be hanging lower than the first.

This is the safest way to hold a hold and puts the least amount of strain on your fingers. Even though you can hang on for 10 seconds, the holds should still be difficult. The goal is to be almost failing at the last set. An example of a finger workout will be as follows:

Warm up: Easy bouldering

Hold 1: 10 seconds on, 10 seconds off x 3 times

Rest: 2-3 minutes

Hold 2: 10 seconds on, 10 seconds off x 3 times

Rest: 2-3 minutes

Hold 3: 10 seconds on, 10 seconds off x 3 times

Rest: 2-3 minutes

Hold 4: 10 seconds on, 10 seconds off x 3 times

Rest: 2-3 minutes

Hold 5: 10 seconds on, 10 seconds off x 3 times

Rest: 2-3 minutes

Hold 6: 10 seconds on, 10 seconds off x 3 times

Cool Down: Stretch

This will be hard, but you shouldn't be sweating, breathing hard, or be super pumped. If you are, rest longer between each set. You should feel completely rested before moving on to the next set. Do this workout once or twice a week with at least 48 hours in between to allow your fingers and tendons to rest. When the holds you are currently on start to feel too easy, up your game. Pick a new hold that is more difficult, but still within the range previously described.

Before you hop on the hangboard, it is imperative that you have the proper technique so you don't injure yourself. It's not a good idea to jump on and just hang. You don't want to injure the rest of your body just to get your fingers strong. Don't be in such a rush to get stronger. This process takes time. Do it properly, it will be better in the long run. So, what is the proper technique for a hangboard?

1. Elbows should be slightly bent; hanging on straight arms could lead to unnecessary strains on the elbow
2. Engage back muscles; shoulders back and down, squeezing the shoulder blades together. This will also engage the shoulders and protect it from injury
3. Head in a neutral position with the eyes facing forward
4. Keep the core tight and supported

Although I say this is the technique for hangboards, this is how the body needs to be engaged for any exercise that requires hanging weight on the arms.

Campusing, in climbing, means to move up a climb without the use of your legs. Essentially you are doing pull ups and/or using momentum to get up the wall. Very rarely do you find it necessary to campus a move on an actual climb, but it is a great form of training to build power and strength in the upper body. As you can imagine, this puts a good deal of stress on the upper body and is recommended you use proper technique to avoid injury.

The proper technique for the campus board is the same as the hangboard. In the climbing gym, you will see some climbers running up the campus board like a ladder. While this looks really cool, it is not as easy as it looks. The simplest workout would be on the largest rungs on the board. Starting with both hands on the same rung, your back and arms engaged, move one arm up to the next rung and come back down, then repeat with the other arm. Do this a couple of times. Rest. Go back to the same starting rung (rung 1), move one hand up to rung 2, then the other hand up to rung 3, like climbing a ladder. If you have to catch rung 2 before you go up to rung 3 with the other hand, that is ok too. Come down and do the same thing, starting with the opposite hand. Like any workout, **warm up** well and **cool down** after with some stretches to work out the lactic acid for a more efficient recovery.

I mentioned this before, but I am going to reiterate because of how important this note is. Do not be in a rush to get your fingers strong fast. Tendons do not build strength the same way muscles do. It takes much longer for them to get stronger and they have a much longer recovery time if anything is to happen to them. I have popped a tendon in my finger once, and I was out for 6 months. It was not worth it.

Endurance Training

There are usually two types of climbers, those who rope up, and those who boulder. Essentially, they are divided into two categories; power and endurance, but the focus should be on becoming a well rounded climber. That way, on the higher climbs, you are able to keep your composure in order to make difficult moves rather than just muscling through. When you are on a long route, you can basically break it down to an x amount of boulder problems. They might not be difficult problems individually, but when you link them together one right after another with minimal rest in between, it becomes a completely new challenge. Not to mention having to clip your rope or place a piece of gear. Think of it this way. If you can run a mile in 8 minutes, keeping that pace for about a mile or two is no big deal but if you run for 10+ miles, it will be difficult to keep that rate. Your legs will start to burn and your knees will feel like buckling, the same concept for your forearms in climbing. Being well rounded and working on endurance will also mean being able to have more than just a few strong attempts at hard boulder problems.

The nature of climbing requires both strength endurance, also known as power endurance and intensive endurance.

- Strength/power endurance allows the climber to better deal with being anaerobic for extended periods of time
- Intensive endurance helps in improving low end endurance and to improve the ability to recover from anaerobic training modes by improving aerobic capacity according to Steve Bechtel in his book <u>Climb Strong Logical Progression</u>.

Just like strength training, the best way to build climbing endurance is to climb more and to climb longer problems. But what happens when the climbing gym is strictly a bouldering gym and does not have high walls to climb on? For all around endurance, traversing is a wonderful way to rack up climbing mileage when walls are short. This is also a great chance to work on technique and footwork.

- Traversing is a lateral movement on the wall, so instead of going up and down, directional movement will be left and right.

A traverse is also excellent as a warm up and cool down. Since traversing will generally be close to the ground in the gym, it could be a fun time to try and work on interesting moves that you have encountered, eliminating the height factor.

Training for Strength/Power Endurance involves interval workouts that will leave you peeling off the wall. We will go over an example of an endurance training session that can be done on the climbing wall.

Example of an interval session on the Climbing wall:

Choose about 6 boulder problems at your onsight level that are about 10-15 moves long.

- Onsight level is the most difficult level of climb you can just walk up to and do in one attempt.

If the climbs in your gym are not 10-15 moves, down climbing or traversing can be done to add moves.

Warm up: Bouldering up to your onsight level, or some sort of body weight exercises to get the blood flowing

You will have 3 minutes to complete each climb and rest before moving on to the next climb. If it takes you 30 seconds to complete the climb, you have 2 minutes and 30- seconds to rest before you start the next climb. After the 6th climb, rest for about 5-10 minutes then start the next round. The workout will be a total of 3 rounds.

- On a 3 minute clock:
- 0:00 Problem 1, then rest
- 3:00 Problem 2, then rest
- 6:00 Problem 3, then rest
- 9:00 Problem 4, then rest
- 12:00 Problem 5, then rest
- 15:00 Problem 6, then rest 5-10 minutes

- Repeat two more times

Training intense endurance will increase your aerobic capacity and your ability to climb higher grades before getting pumped which means getting into anaerobic territory. This type of training is less intense than strength endurance and is usually teetering in the medium to low level of intensity. Instead of focusing on harder moves, the focus of this training will be volume. The difficulty of the workout comes from the duration of time on the wall. The climbs themselves should be well below your onsight level (the highest grade you can walk up to and send in one try). You will be tired after each set, but you should be able to recover to continue on to the next round.

The goal of this workout is to be on the wall for 10 minutes. Use this as an opportunity to practice basic movement skills and practice precision. Movement on the wall can involve climbing up, down climbing and traversing. After 10 minutes are up, rest for 5-10 minutes before repeating 3 more times for a total of 4 sets; 40 minutes wall time. You want to be as fresh as possible before starting each set.

A couple endurance sessions a week on top of strength training and bouldering will work most aspects of climbing to make you a well rounded climber. You will be able to climb more efficiently, sustain longer climbing sessions, and train your body to recover more quickly.

Chapter 5: Injury Prevention

With any sport or activity that puts a lot of strain on the body, comes potential injury. The goal is to reach your ultimate potential without compromising the health of your muscles, joints and tendons. Climbing is no exception. This sport is extremely strenuous on your fingers, elbows, and shoulders in particular, but is not exclusive to them.

Common Climbing Injuries

When it comes to climbing, you would think falling off the wall and landing on your face, especially since the sport entails scaling a vertical (and sometimes overhanging) wall is where all of the damage happens, but most of the injuries happen while you are still hanging on. The following are the most common injuries found in climbing. Some are worse than others, but all of them will take you out of the game for a while to recover.

Pulley Tears

As mentioned before, there are no muscles in the fingers, just tendons and ligaments, making them very vulnerable under stress. This happens when a finger tendon, aka pulley, bears more weight than it is capable, and the climber will hear a pop as soon as it happens followed by pain and swelling. Pulley injuries occur most often in the middle finger and ring finger, and usually happens off a crimp (small holds that are less than a finger pad wide). While a pulley injury is a pain, it is one of the less severe injuries, but you will be out of commission for a solid few months. The best thing to do in the event of a pulley injury is to stop climbing for up to 9 months. If you suspect the injury to be severe, it is recommended to go see a doctor, but many climbers have recovered after resting, icing and massaging/stretching the injured area. When massaging the finger, be sure to gently follow the direction of the tendon, not pull it side to side. To prevent this from happening, allow your tendons time to adapt and practice increasing your crimp strength to ensure your fingers can handle the load you put on them. If you have a strong upper body and can muscle your way through climbs, it will only get you so far. The harder the climb, the smaller the holds or bigger the moves and your tendons will not be able to keep up.

Rotator Cuff Tears

A rotator cuff tear in the shoulder is probably the most common climbing injury, and is one of the most debilitating even in everyday life. The next area of the body that bears the most weight after the fingers are the shoulders. In climbing, the arms are extended above our heads to perform several static and dynamic movements that put a lot of stress on the rotator cuff. There will not always be a popping sound like in the occurrence of a pulley tear, but you will know when it happens. You will feel a sharp pain and an aching sensation in your upper arms and shoulder area and probably won't be able to lift your arm too high without feeling the pain. Your upper arm and shoulder will feel weak and heavy, like there is a lead weight pulling down on the area. For a minor tear, the best thing to do is rest and ice. It goes without saying, stop climbing and keep your arm below shoulder level. Avoid raising your arms above your head and any activity that may be jarring to the rotator cuff. If it still hurts after a few days, it is best to go see a doctor as you may have a more serious tear. The best way to prevent this injury from happening is to stretch the muscles surrounding the rotator cuff and to build the muscles in the areas surrounding to support and stabilize. Also be sure to keep your back engaged whilst climbing so not all the weight and strain goes on the shoulder.

Tendonitis and Tendinosis

Tendonitis means inflamed tendons. Climbers spend a lot of time hanging on and pulling their arms. It is the nature of the sport and is inevitable even with good technique and the use of the legs. The most common areas where tendonitis will form is in the shoulders and elbows. Tendonitis in the shoulder is common due to repeated movement that causes microtrauma over time rather than just one off chance trauma like a tear. With arms above the heads, constantly bearing weight, the pinching of the tendons between the bones in the shoulder over time will also cause swelling and become inflamed.

Medial Epicondylitis, also known as golfer's elbow is a common tendinosis that occurs on the inside of the elbow. If you stand when your arms at your side, palms out, the area of the elbow closest to the body is the site of injury. All the flexors of the fingers and the pronator muscles of the forearms insert in the medial epicondyle, so excessive gripping, or over gripping will add unnecessary stress to this area causing it to inflame.

On the other side of the elbow, is the injury site for Lateral Epicondylitis, also known as tennis elbow. While this is not as common for rock climbers, it is still a possible injury due to all the stress climbers put on their arm.

Like any other injury, the best thing to do is rest and ice. If you continue to climb, be sure to stretch and warm the area very well before climbing. An added brace, or elbow strap can be used to counter force the tendons to reduce strain and protect the area from further injury. As far as injury prevention, work on increasing grip strength, as well as forearm strength, and stretching is critical.

Partial Dislocation

This happens more often in bouldering. You're on the climb that has a big move, somewhat dynamic, or maybe it is a full on dyno, you hit the hold and BAM! You have a searing pain in the back of your shoulders…. Bad news, the ball joint in your shoulder has extended too far forward and all the surrounding muscles and tendons are severely over stress. Not to mention, the shoulder is a bit out of its socket. This one requires the assistance of a physical therapist and health care professional and you are off the wall for a good long while. There will be no climbing as long as the pain persists, unfortunately. You want to prevent this injury, as well as all the other injury, at all costs. When making ANY dynamic or large movements, it is imperative to engage the shoulder and back muscles to protect the shoulder joint and keep the area stable. You should never grab on to any hold with loose shoulders. Relaxed, but never loose, always engaged.

Working Opposing Muscles

Working on opposing muscles, also called antagonistic muscles, is significantly more important than people give it credit for. These muscles are exactly as they are named, they do the opposite of the working muscle. For example: let's say you do a bicep curl, the muscles in the bicep shorten, and the muscles in the triceps lengthen in order to allow this movement. In this case, the bicep is the working muscle, and the tricep is the opposing muscle. If you work on a lot of abdominal strength, besure to balance out by working on the back muscles. Opposing muscles are often neglected, and it is no wonder athletes are getting injured. When it comes to injury prevention, most experts will agree that building overall strength and flexibility in the areas not often used will help avoid injuries.

As a climber, pulling muscles are put into overdrive and are getting stronger with every session. The more you climb, the tighter those muscles get, and eventually you are the hunchback of notre dame and your posture is terrible. Many of the muscles in the upper body, including the latissimus dorsi, pull your shoulders forward as it tightens, leaving them in a compromised and unstable position. As the muscles you are working are contracting, the opposite muscles are lengthening and will continuously lengthen to due to the lack of work. Think of it as a rubber band. If these muscles are stretched and stretched, one wrong move and it could snap and you have a pulled muscle. Sounds like a bad time. Not only are your muscles vulnerable, but now you also have one set of muscles pulling harder on your joints than the other. This can torque and pull your joints out of alignment.

Stretching the worked muscles and working the opposing muscles will build strength evenly throughout the body creating a balance and better performance. Balance is crucially important to overall fitness. If you are muscularly imbalanced, you are at risk of injury. If you don't have any flexibility, you are at risk or pulling a muscle that is too tight. If you work one muscle group continuously but neglect to work the opposing muscles, you risk injuring the joints and tendons in that area due to imbalanced support. Work those antagonists!! This applies to the entire body, not just the arms.

Here are some great opposing muscle workouts for climbing. Do these a few times a week.

- Shoulder Press

- Push-up
- Bench Press
- Dips
- Reverse wrist curl
- External Rotation of the shoulders
- Internal Rotation of the shoulders

Yoga is another great supplement to climbing. Not only are you stretching and strengthening muscles making you stronger and more limber, but it incorporates a solid amount of opposing muscle work. Yoga also teaches you how to effectively use your breath which is very helpful on the wall. How you control your breath can calm you down on the wall, or give you that extra umph to make a move. We sometimes forget how important breathing is and how much controlling it can make you more efficient on the wall. If you have never done yoga before, it is something to consider.

Tendons vs Muscles

By definition, a tendon or sinew is a tough band of fibrous connective tissue that connects muscle to bone and serves to move the bone. Essentially, when you move, your muscles contract or lengthen, pulling on tendons which then pulls on the bones producing movement. They also act as rubber bands that stretch and shorten to absorb impact during activities; like natural shock absorbers. The downside to these amazing fibers is they receive less blood flow than muscles. Less blood means slower recovery and repair. The strength that muscles can build in days would takes weeks, even months for the tendons.

Warm up, Cool Down, Stretch

Warming up, cooling down and stretching is considered to be boring and are often forgotten or ignored. I am here to tell you, if you want to lower your risk of injury, these three activities are the absolute foundation.

Warming Up

The first thing you should do before any workout is warm up, and climbing is no different. And I don't mean climbing a couple easy climbs and calling it a day before you jump on your projects. From your fingertips down to your toes, you'll need to get every part of your body prepared for what you are about to subject it to. Here is a sample warm up before even considering getting on the wall:

1. Fingers - Since the fingers only have tendons there is very little blood flow into the area, so by doing this you are forcing some blood flow to warm up the fingers
    a. Hold your hands in a tight fist for a couple of seconds, then shoot the fingertips out, flex and hold for another couple of seconds - repeat 10 times

2. Wrists - Wrists are exposed to their fullest range of motion and they should be warmed up as such. Start on hands and knees, arms shoulder width apart
    a. Palms facing down directly under shoulders - lean forward until you feel the stretch on the medial (inner) part of your forearms and hold
    b. Palms still facing down, rotate the hands inward and outward, holding the stretches in between
    c. Palms facing upward - flip your hands so that you are now resting on the top part of your hands, and lean back towards your heels - you will feel this on the lateral (outer) part of your forearms
    d. Palms still upward, rotate the hands inward and outward, holding the stretches in between
3. Elbows - Often the most forgotten area to stretch and see the most injuries
    a. Find a wall. Palms against the wall below shoulder line, outwardly rotated until the finger tips are pointing down and inner elbow is facing up
        i. Bracing against the wall, lift the inner elbow towards the sky until you feel a stretch in the bicep
        ii. Switch sides

4. Shoulders - Next to the wrists, shoulders are exposed to and thrown into all sorts of angles. Mobility is vital
    a. Laterally extend arms out shoulder height and flex the wrists like you are about to shoot lasers from the palms of your hands
        i. Draw 10 circles forward
        ii. Draw 10 circles backward
    b. Scapular pull-ups - find something to hang on: hang board, pull up bar, rings. Etc
        i. Begin in a normal pull up position
        ii. From a full hang with slightly shrugged shoulders, without bending your arms, engage your lats and draw your scapula down together and squeeze
        iii. Repeat 5-10 times
        iv. Try with a wider grip
5. Hips and Hamstrings - Remember, climbing is in the hips and the legs, make sure they are warm
    a. Stand with one foot forward and one foot back, heels in line, back foot slightly out turned
    b. Flex front foot, pulling toes towards you, bend back leg and with a straight back, bend forward leading with your chest.
    c. Hold for 15 seconds

d. Bring palms together in the inside of your forward foot, with a flat back, open outer arm towards the sky, opening your chest away from your foot
   e. Repeat 10 times
   f. Switch sides
6. Calves and Feet - This goes without saying. Your calves and feet are your foundation
   a. Calf raises - slow and controlled
      i. 10 reps
7. Ankles - Full of tendons, and little muscle, don't forget to warm these bad boys up and get the blood flowing
   a. Ankle rolls
      i. 10 in each direction

Cool Down

As I mentioned before, this is another crucial part of the climbing day that is almost always forgotten. Having done some hard climbs, your have put your body through a lot of stress. Cooling down does a number of things:

1. Helps the body repair muscle fibers, tendons and ligaments that may have been damaged
2. Keeps the blood circulating and regulates blood flow back to a pre-workout state
3. Relaxes the body and decreases the heart rate
4. Removes toxin build-up from muscles

Some examples of cooling down would be:

1. Easy, slow climbing
2. Light cardio
3. Static Stretching
4. Foam roll
5. Massage sore muscles

Stretching

Before climbing, to warm up the body, you will want to focus on active and dynamic stretching. Active stretching stimulates the muscles and prepares them for use during climbing. Dynamic stretching involves movement in the body to gradually increasing reach, loosening up the joints and muscles before jumping on the wall. Just as the name entails, active and dynamic stretching uses movement to stretch and increase mobility.

After climbing is a good time to incorporate static stretching. Static stretching is a much deeper, slower stretch where you hold a position for 30+ seconds and is best left for after climbing. Doing so before your body is warm could be detrimental. Imagine stretching a frozen rubber band: the band weakens and is not able to support the stress, which is why dynamic stretching is recommended to warm up the body. After a session, static stretches increases flexibility, cools you down, relaxes the muscles and decreases tension in the muscles.

Chapter 6: Be Polite, Don't be a Jerk - Climbing Etiquette

Just like any other society or community, there is a certain code of behavior that is expected of one another. Some of these may seem like common sense, but I cannot tell you how many times I've seen these codes broken. With this huge influx of climbers joining the sport, the number of new climbers is greatly outweighing the number of OG climbers to pass on valuable knowledge. The lack of education is becoming more and more apparent, but you don't have to fall into that category. It's quite simple, really. Be Polite, don't be a jerk! Here are some simple etiquette rules to follow.

"Spraying Beta" and why it is a No No

First of all, what is "beta"? Beta is a term used in climbing to describe how to climb a route. "Spraying beta" means to give information (beta) on how to climb a route without being asked. Now why is this such a no no?

Climbing is a puzzle. The whole idea behind climbing is to figure out how you can get to the top, yourself. For most, that "figuring it out" part is the journey and one that they want to discover for themselves. You shouting out your ideas of how a climb should be done, or how you would do it, is robbing them of their experience of overcoming a challenge on their own.

You are taking away their opportunity to put solve the puzzle themselves. You're cheating them out of their victory. Need I go on? It may sound dramatic, but what if your advice doesn't suit their body or climbing style? What if you're giving them wrong advice? Even if the beta is good beta, zip the lip. You may think you're helping, but this advice is unsolicited and unwanted. Don't do it. It isn't your place to do so. Even good beta spray is bad beta spray. Spray is Spray. Even the word sounds annoying. More often than not, you'll just annoy your fellow climbers. If they want your ideas, they'll ask you.

Should they ask you for your advice, don't tell them what they should and should not do, instead tell them "this is what worked for me" or "here is what I did." When asked, give them references and ideas, but ONLY when asked.

LNT - Leave No Trace

This one is a no brainer. Leave the place as you found it. Being outside is incredible and nature has so much to offer us so treat it with respect. Enjoy the great outdoors with minimal impact and leaving it pristine for the next adventurers to enjoy. Nature is incredible. Do your part in preserving it for generations to come.

- **Pick up your Trash**
  - Everything you bring with you, you take back with you. Don't leave trash lying around, nature is not your trash can.

You wouldn't leave trash in your bed, don't leave it here
  - Did you know that it takes 2 YEARS for a banana peel to decompose?
- **Leave what you find**
  - Find something so beautiful you want to take it home with you? Leave it and allow the next person to experience what you just did.
  - If everyone were to take a piece of nature they liked, the land will end up bare
- **Stay on the Trail**
  - Not only is this for your own safety, but also to preserve the park
  - Trails are maintained and well kempt, leaving it may risk falls and sprains from uneven terrain
  - Going off trail means stepping on plants that could have taken years to grow. You're killing nature, how do you feel about that?
- **Respect the Wildlife**
  - Don't disturb plants or wildlife just to get the perfect picture or selfie. Nature isn't there for you to trample on. It is there for you to admire from afar.
  - Go in smaller groups to minimize your footprint
  - Don't play loud music and startle the animals, not to mention annoy the crap

out of other climbers. You're outside, enjoy the natural music of your surroundings. Some people come out to escape city life and to have peace, don't ruin it for them.
- Don't feed the animals, this could stress them and who knows what they could be carrying
- Be aware of the weather and how that affects the rock
- **You are a guest here, don't run around like you own the place**

First Come, First Serve

Everyone knows this concept. It's nothing new and it isn't exclusive to climbing. Waiting in line at a grocery store; getting seated at a restaurant; setting your towel down at the beach. Showing up at a route or boulder problem is no different. The first person or group to set down their gear at a climb has claim to that area until finished. Same thing if you're in the climbing gym. If you see someone working on a problem, ask them if you can join. Chances are, they won't say no, but it's polite to ask.

While I've seen this happen both on ropes and bouldering, it is more prevalent in bouldering. Let me put together a little scenario: You walk up to a boulder problem, but there are already pads on the ground. This spot is occupied, but this is the problem you've been wanting to climb, what do you do?

    A. Set your stuff down and just start laying out your gear

    B. Ask them if it's cool for you to join them

Answer A is just plain rude, and you wouldn't do that anywhere in society. Even at a bar, you ask the person next to the empty seat if it's cool for you to sit there. Answer B is the way to go. Granted, they aren't going to say no because they know they don't own the space, but it's still polite to ask. Remember? Don't be a jerk. Be respectful to your surroundings, including the people in them. You may think this is silly and obvious, but allow me to tell you about an encounter I had the misfortune of having.

It was a beautiful Saturday afternoon at Black Mountain. The sun was high and the air was crisp. We made our way to the visor boulder to work on Can Opener, a nice crimpy line up the right side of the boulder. After warming up, we laid down our crash pads and took in the fresh air and relished in the peace and quiet. It seemed like we were the only ones on the mountain. And then we heard it... It sounded like an amphitheatre full of people were making their way towards us, and we were not far off. About 25 people talking loudly, music playing, coming right for us. It was an ambush. The large group came up to the boulder, set their pads down and took up the whole area. If you paid attention to the previous section, you will know that this is already a faux pas. 25 is not a small group and loud music is annoying, this isn't a climbing gym. We don't all have the same music taste. Don't assume we want to listen to what you have to play. One person was kind enough to ask if it was cool if they worked on the problem next to us. After the fact, but at least they asked. Of course, we weren't going to say no.

Then, one guy walked over to the climb my friend and I were working on, stepped on our pads, and touched all of the holds with his greasy un-chalked hands. Goes without saying, we were extremely agitated and pissed. Two things here:

1. If a crash pad is not yours, don't step all over it without asking permission. You don't go and touch other people's things without asking, a crash pad is no different.
2. Touching the rock with un-chalked hands spreads all of the oil from the skin onto the rock making it more slick and polished. When a climb is already difficult with small holds, we don't need to make it even harder. Chalk your hands

A couple of his friends noticed our frustration, we weren't exactly hiding it, caught his attention and apologized for him. Your friend's shouldn't have to apologize for you, be cognizant, don't be that person.

Because of this, the rest of the day, our energy and excitement was low. The whole situation killed the mood. We made sure not to mention where we were going next, afraid the group would somehow follow us. Imagine how you would feel if you would feel if your personal space was invaded by a large number of people. Not great, right? So avoid doing so yourself, it's just bad form.

Be Present

Be aware of what is going on around you. Climbing can be a very dangerous sport if you are not paying attention and going about your day with your head in the clouds. Every aspect of climbing requires a great deal of focus, whether you are on or off the wall.

When you are on the wall, every thought that goes through your head translates into your movements, even if you don't realize it.

- You don't trust your foot? Then subconsciously you won't transfer enough weight onto your foot and your foot will blow off.
- Don't trust the hold you're going to? You won't commit to the move and come off the wall.
- Not focusing on your breathing and engaging your muscles? You are going to flail on the wall and possibly injure yourself.
- What do plan on having for dinner? What you want to do tomorrow? All of this takes the focus off your climbing and you are likely to slip up

These are just a few examples of what could be going on in your head. There are already so many natural factors that are out of your control; it's humid, it's hot, the holds are greasy. Control what you can, your body. Climbing is like a meditation. Once your feet leave the ground, nothing else matters except you and the climb.

Being off the wall doesn't mean you can go off and day dream, you have other factors to contend with.

- Spotting a friend? Make sure your hands and body are in the proper position to catch them in the event they fall. Know your surroundings so that you don't take a fall and that anything protruding is covered. Make sure there are no gaps between the pads. I have a few sprained ankles under my belt because my spotter wasn't paying attention. It is not something to be proud of. Be sure you have done everything you can to ensure you and the climber are safe.
- Belaying a partner? I mentioned this before, and I will say this again because it is critical. You are holding your partner's life in your hands. There is a lot to think about and can risk serious injury if your head isn't in the game.

  - Give them enough slack
  - Don't short rope them
  - Be ready when they fall
  - Listen to what they are telling you

I've had a friend get dropped to the ground from high up on ropes because the belayer's head was somewhere else. This wasn't an inexperienced belayer either, it could happen to anyone. PAY ATTENTION

Doing neither of these things and just walking around. Whether you are in the climbing gym or outdoors, there are obstacles everywhere you can trip over or bump into. Especially bouldering at the gym, be mindful of the people on the wall. Don't just walk under them. If they fall, both of you will get injured. The person on the wall should not have to get injured for your mindlessness. Look up, look down, know what's around you. I get it, climbing is a fun and social sport, and it is easy to get caught up in everything but safety is always first.

Unwritten Rules of Climbing

Follow these unwritten rules and you'll have a great time and make it enjoyable for those climbing around you:

- Leave no trace
- Erase your tick marks
- Don't beta spray - don't feel obligated to teach
- Don't chip or drill holds
- Not yours? DON'T Touch
- Be mindful of sound - don't play loud music
- Don't hog routes
- Don't rush others
- Be encouraging and motivating
- Be respectful
- Don't brag

Chapter 7: Transitioning Outside

Climbing in the gym is fun, but climbing outdoors is the the full experience. Many climbers use the gym as a training tool for the real deal; real rock. It's no longer about just climbing. It's about the adventure, the view, the fresh air. It's peaceful yet unpredictable. Something about being outside lifts this weight off your shoulders, even for just that moment. If you're an outdoor person that is. If you are not, that's ok too, it's still an experience. Being outside is fantastic, but it also introduces a slew of other elements to be conscious of.

Can I Climb Alone?

While climbing is a social sport, it is not always easy to find someone who can make the trek outside with you, or sometimes you just want to be alone, which is why bouldering is such an appealing discipline. Most boulders are less than 30 feet tall and all that is needed is a crash pad, chalk and shoes. In sport, lead, or trad climbing, it goes without saying, you need a partner in order to do anything.

Although you CAN go climbing outdoors alone and many people do, for safety reasons, it's always a good idea to have at least one person with you when you adventure outside the safety of four walls. At minimum, tell someone where you are going. Landing zones are not always the best and climbs are not always a direct line straight up. Anything could happen and safety is never guaranteed. You are most likely going to a remote location with no cellular service and even something like a twisted ankle could be very dangerous. Even if you are extremely careful, the elements are unpredictable and unforgiving. Imagine if any of these events occur and you are alone:

- Take a bad fall
- Slip and sprain your ankle
- Get lost
- Hit your head

A partner will spot you on the climb and help prevent these things from happening. They can move the pad directly under you as you move. A spotter can guide you onto your pad if you fall. Yes, you can climb alone, but weigh the risks. If you intend on climbing by yourself, it is a lot safer to do so in a climbing gym where the whole ground is covered in thick pad.

Most Common Types of Rock

Not all rock is the same. There are so many different types of rocks to be climbed on and they each have their own unique characteristics. It is important to know the properties of the rock you are climbing and how weather affects it. Each rock type has a different hardness and is weathered into different shapes and formations creating beautifully unique lines for us to reap the benefits of.

Granite

Granite is the most common igneous rock, which originates from magma and lava, on earth and form some of the most renowned climbing mechas in the world; Yosemite and Joshua Tree in California and Mount Rushmore in South Dakota to name a few. This type of igneous rock is plutonic and covers nearly 100% of the earth's crust (both on land and underwater) and is eroded to form the faces we dream of climbing. Granite is a course, rough rock that is light in color. Depending on the minerals in the granite, colors can range from a white-ish grey, to oranges and pinks. Granite generally contains a higher content of quartz and feldspar which makes it hard and resistant to erosion.

The sharp minerals found in granite gives the rock a rough texture that bites into any surface it touches, whether it be climbing shoes or skin. Granite formations are generally large, strong and imposing with poor permeability. Meaning the rock is not porous and does not soak up much water after a rainfall. Weakness lie in the fractures. Water will run through any cracks and fractures present, eroding and widening the gaps creating some of the most astounding crack climbs in the world.

Limestone

Limestone is a type of sedimentary rock rich in a salt called calcium carbonate. This type of sedimentary rocks are a type of rock formed by the collection of deposits of minerals and organic particles found on the floors of oceans or other bodies of water on the earth's surface. Over time this sediment is pressurized and cemented together to form what we have the pleasure of climbing today.

Generally light in color, limestone is usually found in caves composed of the skeletal remains of marine organisms like coral that have left their shells behind . Crazy right? Think about it the next time you climb on limestone. Where you are standing, used to be under the ocean. Limestone is very hard durable, providing a great surface for climbing. Acid from rainfall can slowly dissolve the limestone creating different ever changing features. Limestone also absorbs oils from the skin and becomes smooth over time. You will notice that climbs that see more traffic will be slick and feel like someone poured epoxy all over it.

Limestone forms some of the most unique climbing features around the world. Some of the most famous limestone crags are: Mount Charleston in Las Vegas, Ceuse in France, Dolomites in Italy, and Verdon Gorge in France to name a few.

Sandstone

Sandstone is another type of sedimentary rock that is formed under different circumstances than limestone and covers about 75% of the earth's surface making it the most common rock on the earth's surface. Sandstone is formed when small sand sized mineral particles and minute rock fragments that are swept up by running water begin to accumulate and settle on the ground surface. As more sand is accumulated, the weight of the overlying deposits compressed and cemented the sediment precipitating minerals and hardens into what we know as sandstone.

If you have ever been to or seen pictures of the Grand Canyon, you will see the layers upon layers of sediment that have laid to rest over the millions of years. Due to the nature of how sandstone is created, it is the most fragile of rocks currently being climbed on. It is soft, easily eroded and very porous. Sandstone is like a sponge. After a full day of rain, you should wait at least 3-4 days before climbing on sandstone. Even if the rock can look dry the day after a heavy rain, chances are there is a lot of moisture in its pores. If the ground around the rock is wet, definitely do NOT climb. You risk breaking the holds breaking the rock, injuring yourself, and ruining the climb for all your fellow climbers. I'll warn you now, you'll get a lot of hate.

While Sandstone is a softer rock, it has great friction and your hands won't hurt as bad as it would after a day of climbing on granite.

Some of the greatest sandstone climbing can be found at Indian Creek Canyon and Moab in Utah, Red Rocks in Las Vegas, Zion National Park in Utah, and Badami in India.

Volcanic

Volcanic rock is another type of igneous rock formed from the cooling of magma and lava. The features of volcanic rock are sharp and pitted, formed from the bubbling of magma while cooling.

This type of rock is sturdy and have a variety of features.

- Vesicular Basalt - Jagged, Sharp, and extremely painful to hold
- Micro-Crystalline Basalt - Smooth and Glassy
- Pharentic or Combination - Comfortable enough to hold

Rarely are these climbs slab. Various pockets can be found on vertical or overhanging routes.

Some places to find this type of rock would be: all over the Hawaiian Islands, Happys and Sads in Bishop California, and Sonora Pass in California.

Multi-pitch and Big Wall Climbing

Half Dome, El Capitan, Ulvetana Queen Maud Land. Welcome to the world of Big Wall Climbing. Some of the most epic faces in the world tower over thousands of feet. Walls so tall, humans look like ants if you have the eyes of a hawk and can manage to spot them. One rope length isn't going to get you anywhere near the top. A pitch is a single length of climbing up to a set of anchors. At these anchors, in a single pitch climb, the climber would set the anchors and get lowered. In a multi-pitch climb - a climb with more than one length of climbing and multiple anchor stations, the lead climber would climb to the first set of anchors, lock themselves in, and belay the follower from the top. The following climber will need to clean the gear - the act of removing all the pieces of gear placed by the leader. Once both climbers are at the same set of anchors, they will continue in the same fashion up to the next set of anchors, and to the next, to the next, until they reach the top.

A multi-pitch climb just means any climb that has more than one pitch and cannot be completed with one length of rope. Generally, a suggested rope length for the outdoors is 70 meters and an average pitch length is 100 feet but can range anywhere from 20 feet to 200 feet. Not everyone is ready to spend more than one day on a large 31 pitch climb like El Capitan, but there are plenty of incredible multi-pitch climbs all around the world ranging in all difficulties for you to get in your vertical miles.

Most multi-pitch climbs will require trad gear and skills. This means you will have to build your own anchors. Rope management and communication is of utmost importance. Rope management is tedious, but with practice, the correct coiling of the rope saves time and makes life much easier. Dealing with a tangled rope hundreds of feet in the air is a nightmare. Communication is not going to be easy. Stakes are much higher when you're, well... higher. Mistakes can be disastrous and fatal, so you are going to want to avoid those at all costs. You and your partner need to have some sort of communication system or plan worked out on the ground before you tie yourselves in. If pitches are short, you'll be able to shout at each other, but when pitches are long, you won't be so lucky. And on a windy day, good luck hearing yourself shout. You will need a way to tell one another when you're anchored in, ready to climb, when you can be taken off belay, etc, etc. Any of these can end in disaster if done prematurely. Be safe.

A lot more preparation goes in to a multi-pitch climb. More than likely, you will be on the wall all day. That means you will need to carry food and water with you on the wall. Study the route. Know where it starts, where it moves, where it ends, and it will be a good idea to have the topos with you as you climb. How many pitches is it? How long should it take? What does the descent look like? There is no such thing as being over prepared.

Take it from me. I have made the mistake of not being well informed about the descent, and my partners and I got lost going down. We had to find the way down, in the dark on loose ground. Safe to say, that mistake was never made again, but we were lucky. It could have ended poorly for us. Do not make that same mistake. Go with experienced climbers who can show you the ropes, pun intended.

The "Approach"

What is the "approach"? You'll hear this often associated with climbing outside, whether it be bouldering or rope climbing. To put it simply, the approach is the hike from your car or campsite to the base of the climb. This could take anywhere from 2 minutes to 2 hours, maybe longer, who knows.

Climbers dread a long approach. Hiking is one thing, but hiking with 30-40lbs of gear on your back, plus the rope is an ordeal. To make things more uncomfortable, the terrain is not always flat. Honestly, sometimes you'll already be tuckered out before you even start to climb! The dream is to be able to step out of your car and have the route right in front of you, but alas, rocks didn't shape and place themselves for our benefit. We want to climb something spectacular? We have to work for it.

Occasionally, the approach will require some scrabbling and light easy climbing to get to where you need to go. Where standard hiking shoes may not be secure for such situations, in comes the approach shoe, aptly named for its function. Approach shoes are hiking shoes made with climbing rubber for that extra stickiness needed without having to slip on your climbing shoes. Many approach shoes are so good, they could be to climb.

Climbing After a Rainy Day

Easy... DON'T

After a full day of rain, it is never a good idea to hop on a rock, for your safety and for the preservation of the rock. You will get a bunch of hate from the community, and if I were to be honest, it wouldn't be because they feared for your safety. You are risking the integrity of the climb, and could very well be destroying it for everyone else. To the rest of the community, you are ruining their climb.

Good rules of thumb for climbing after the rain:

- On Sandstone:
    - Wait at least 24 hours after a moderate shower
    - Wait up to 48 hours after a day of heavy shower
    - After multiple days of heavy showers, you could be waiting for up to a week
    - Remember, sandstone is like a sponge, soaks up all the moisture and loses strength when wet. Even if it looks dry, it is still fragile from the rain
    - If the ground base is wet, DO NOT CLIMB
- On Granite:
    - Generally impermeable and dries quickly after rain
    - Granite isn't porous so the water usually runs right off
    - Usually the rock of choice after rain
    - After light showers, you don't really have to wait to climb, but it is at your own risk
    - After heavy rain, 24 hours should suffice
- On Limestone:
    - Limestone gets slimy after rain, but also dries pretty quickly after rain
    - After heavy rain, it is always smart to wait 24 hours before climbing, for the safety of the rock

- If the ground is still wet, then there is possible moisture on the rock and it is ill advised to climb

It is simple really, don't be so gung-ho to climb that you risk potentially breaking holds and robbing the climb from everybody else. It makes you selfish. You can wait, the rock isn't going anywhere.

ABC's of Climbing Index

Some, but not all, climbing lingo to remember

A. Arete - an edge or ridge where two walls meet

B. Back Step - stepping on a hold with the outside edge of the shoe, and pivoting the hip into the wall, ie: outside edge of right shoe on hold, right hip into the wall

C. Choss - A climb or hold can be considered "chossy" if it is grainy and poor quality

D. Deck - to hit the ground on a fall; typically a rope term

E. Edging - using the edge of the climbing shoe whilst climbing

F. Flash - sending a climb in one go, after having received beta of some kind

G. Gaston - a style of gripping a hold with your elbows out and thumbs down and applying pressure towards the elbow

H. Heel Hook - applying pressure on a hold with the back of the heel and pulling the heel in towards the butt

I. Ice Screw - long tubular screw used as protection in ice climbing

J. Jug - a large hold that is easy to hold on to

K. Knee Bar - using your leg (from the knee down to the foot) as a cam between two protruding sections of rock

L. Lock off - using body tension to hold one arm in a bent position in order to reach the next hold with the other arm

M. Mantle - a technique used to go over a ledge or feature on a rock that lacks any holds; using the palms of your hands to push down to lift the body instead of using fingers to pull the body up

N. Nut - a metal wedge that slides into a crack for protection in trad climbing

O. Onsight - finishing a climb with no falls or prior knowledge of the climb; no beta or practice

P. Punting - when the climber falls off the easy moves on a hard climb

Q. Quickdraw - a type of protection used in sport climbing comprised of two carabiners connected by strong webbing. One end to clip the wall, and the other to clip the rope

R. Redpoint - Finishing a clean without taking a fall after having practiced the route beforehand

S. Sloper - a rounded surface on a rock that requires the friction of your whole hand to stay on

T. Testpiece - the hardest climb for the grade in any given area

U. Undercling - a hold that requires the climber to grip with the palms facing upwards

V. Volume - A large, hollow hold commonly used in bouldering gyms; generally made of plywood

W. Whipper - a dramatic, long distance fall taken by a lead climber with a force great enough to lift the belayer

X. Xeno - a hold that looks like it is a different type of rock compared to the rest of the wall

Y. Yabo - sit start; "Yabo start"

Z. Z-Clip - in lead climbing, grabbing the rope from beneath the last piece of protection to clip in to the next piece of protection

About the Expert

Brigitte has been competitive athlete since a very young age and in those years she learned how imperative it is to allow the body to adapt to each sport. In college, she competed in Water Polo, Swimming and was on the NCAA Div 2 Women's Crew Team at University of California San Diego. Having a strong foundation is key in any sport, and climbing is no different. Brigitte has been climbing for about 10 years and throughout her climbing career, she was fortunate enough to have amazing mentors and experienced climbers pass their invaluable knowledge down to her and she wants to do her part in passing it all to you. You can learn more about Brigitte and her rock climbing journey at www.instagram.com/cartastrophe.

HowExpert publishes quick 'how to' guides on all topics from A to Z by everyday experts. Visit HowExpert.com to learn more.

Recommended Resources

- HowExpert.com – Quick 'How To' Guides on All Topics from A to Z by Everyday Experts.
- HowExpert.com/free – Free HowExpert Email Newsletter.
- HowExpert.com/books – HowExpert Books
- HowExpert.com/courses – HowExpert Courses
- HowExpert.com/membership – HowExpert Membership Site
- HowExpert.com/writers – Write About Your #1 Passion/Knowledge/Expertise & Become a HowExpert Author.
- HowExpert.com/resources – Additional HowExpert Recommended Resources
- YouTube.com/HowExpert – Subscribe to HowExpert YouTube.
- Instagram.com/HowExpert – Follow HowExpert on Instagram.
- Facebook.com/HowExpert – Follow HowExpert on Facebook.

Made in the USA
Las Vegas, NV
15 November 2020